Artful
Jewish Designs
COLORING BOOK

Miryam Adatto

Dover Publications, Inc.
Mineola, New York

Judaism is full of beautiful, beloved symbols and motifs from holidays and daily life. This book features religious objects, including a mezuzah and Torah scrolls, as well as familiar images like peace doves and the Jerusalem cityscape. There are abundant Stars of David with a wide range of creative details and patterns. Celebrate Rosh Hashanah with apples and honey, Hanukkah with a menorah and dreidel, and Passover with a seder plate. Specially designed for the experienced colorist, the illustrations in this book offer an escape to a world of inspiration and artistic fulfillment. Each of the thirty-one plates has been perforated for removal to make displaying your work easy.

Copyright

Copyright © 2018 by Dover Publications, Inc.
All rights reserved.

Bibliographical Note

Artful Jewish Designs Coloring Book is a new work, first published by Dover Publications, Inc., in 2018.

International Standard Book Number

ISBN-13: 978-0-486-82854-1
ISBN-10: 0-486-82854-9

Manufactured in the United States by LSC Communications
82854901   2018
www.doverpublications.com

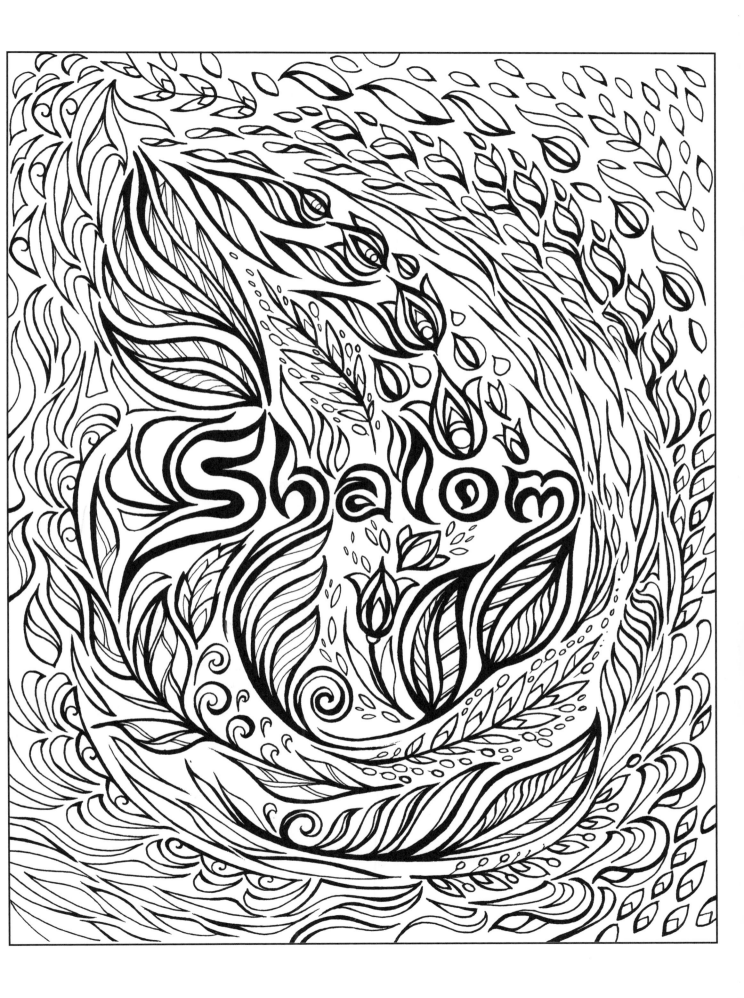